"Soaring to New Heights"

Self-Acceptance

Building Confidence

by Robert Wandberg, PhD

Consultants:
Roberta Brack Kaufman, EdD
Dean, College of Education
Concordia University
St. Paul, Minnesota

Millie Shepich, MPH, CHES
Health Educator and District Health Coordinator
Waubonsie Valley High School
Aurora, Illinois

"Soaring to New Heights"

LifeMatters
an imprint of Capstone Press
Mankato, Minnesota

Thank you to the students of the Hennepin County Home School, who provided valuable feedback for the direction this book has taken.

LifeMatters Books are published by Capstone Press
PO Box 669 • 151 Good Counsel Drive • Mankato, Minnesota 56002
http://www.capstone-press.com

Printed in the United State of America

Library of Congress Cataloging-in-Publication Data
Wandberg, Robert.
      Self-acceptance: building confidence / by Robert Wandberg.
          p.   cm. — (Life skills)
      Includes bibliographical references and index.
      ISBN 0-7368-1024-2
      1. Self-acceptance—Juvenile literature. 2. Teenagers—Conduct of life—Juvenile literature.
[1. Self-acceptance.] I. Title. II. Series.
      BF575.S37 W36 2002
      158.1—dc21   00-012918
                                                      CIP

Summary: Describes self-acceptance as a combination of three areas: social, physical, and mental and emotional self-acceptance. Also provides information about accepting one's gifts and disabilities, as well as putting self-acceptance into action.

Staff Credits
Charles Pederson, editor; Adam Lazar, designer; Kim Danger, photo researcher

Photo Credits
Cover: ©Tim Yoon
International Stock/©Scott Barrow, 34
Photo Network/©Henryk T. Kaiser, 8; ©Myrleen Ferguson Cate, 39
Photri Inc/©Fotopic, 11; ©Skjold, 31, 59; ©Jeff Greenberg, 53
Uniphoto-Pictor/©Jackson Smith, 17; ©Mark Reinstein, 48
Unicorn Stock Photos/©Joel Dexter, 24; ©Jeff Greenberg, 26; ©Tommy Dodson, 45; ©Chris Boylan, 54
©Tim Yoon, 5, 15, 23, 33, 41, 51
Visuals Unlimited, Inc., 49

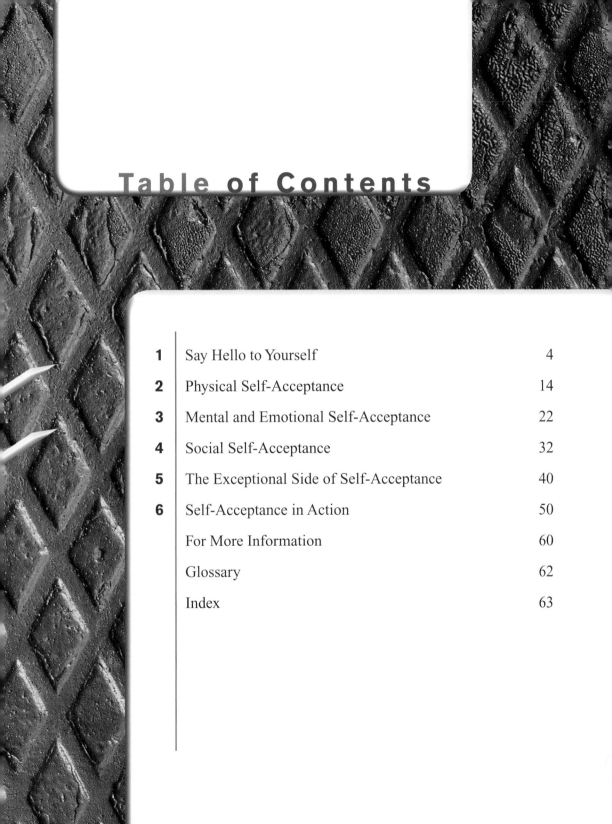

Table of Contents

Chapter Overview

Self-acceptance is appreciation for yourself. Low self-acceptance sometimes leads to risky or destructive behavior. The three parts to self-acceptance are physical, social, and mental and emotional self-acceptance.

Competence and confidence may affect self-acceptance. Confidence may come and go.

High self-acceptance has many benefits.

People may have trouble accepting themselves. Sometimes they base their self-acceptance on whether others accept them. This can lead to problems.

Self-assessments are tests people can take to know themselves better.

Goals

CHAPTER 1

⌂

Say Hello to Yourself

What Is Self-Acceptance?

Self-acceptance is the condition of appreciating and valuing yourself physically, socially, and mentally and emotionally. It might be called **AcceptanceMatters**. Healthy self-acceptance is a skill. Like any skill, it takes work. High self-acceptance may include these characteristics:

Feeling worthy of being happy

Knowing, understanding, and valuing strengths and traits

Knowing, understanding, and improving weaknesses

Knowing that you're lovable and capable

Knowing that you can give and receive friendship and affection

On the other hand, low self-acceptance can be destructive. It's often connected with poor health behaviors. These include alcohol and other drug use, suicide, eating disorders, and high-risk sexual behaviors. Suicide is intentionally killing yourself.

TEEN TALK

"This guy at school, Les, is such a know-it-all. He never listens to anything other people say. Or if he pauses for a second, and someone else does say something, he just ignores them. He might have friends, but no one I know hangs around with him."
—Crista, age 15

One of the first rules of self-acceptance is that only you are responsible for your failures and successes. This book is meant to help you understand and develop self-acceptance. Accepting yourself can become the basis for your values and priorities. Your values and priorities are an important guide for your decisions and behaviors.

Self-acceptance doesn't mean that you dismiss other people's thoughts or beliefs. That might be considered arrogant. Others may see such overconfidence as not being able to change. It could result in social isolation, or having people avoid you.

Parts of Self-Acceptance

Many things influence a person's self-acceptance. Three particular influences are the physical, social, and mental or emotional parts. These parts influence each other, as well. For example, a physical injury may make you sad, angry, or depressed. This, in turn, can make social health difficult. You may not want to see friends. This may affect your mental health. You may feel worried or sad about not seeing your friends. In turn, the worry or sadness may make you physically ill again. Your body may be weak, and you could get sick.

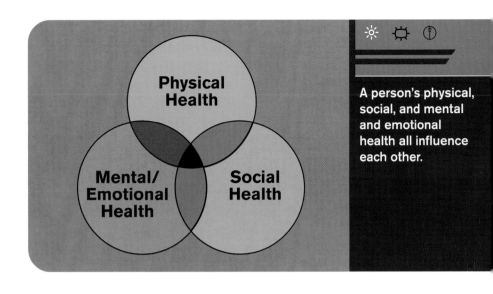

A person's physical, social, and mental and emotional health all influence each other.

Self-Acceptance, Competence, and Confidence

Competence is the ability to cope with life's challenges, including both routine and occasional challenges. Confidence is faith in yourself and your competence. Your confidence can seriously affect your self-acceptance. Confident people believe they can succeed. When a problem arises, they expect to solve it. Athletes often go into a contest expecting to win rather than trying not to lose. There are many challenges and contests besides athletics, such as getting your homework done.

Tim, Age 15

Tim finally tried out for the community play. On the day of the tryout, the drama coach he had been working with was sick. Tim was used to speaking in front of his coach. But now the substitute coach sat in front of him. He wanted to die when the woman said, "Hurry up, I don't have all day." She had no idea how shy Tim was or how hard he had worked. Tim felt his confidence drain away.

Smoking because friends do it is one poor choice that peer pressure may cause teens to make.

It's easy for confidence to come and go. Building confidence isn't always easy, as Tim found out. The more you practice, the stronger your confidence becomes. Remind yourself of your past achievements. This will help boost your confidence. For example, Tim could remember that his regular coach often mentioned how much talent he thought Tim had. When you are competent and confident, you'll likely have high self-acceptance.

What's So Great About Self-Acceptance?

As your self-acceptance increases, you may experience many benefits. You might better understand your feelings and behaviors. This understanding helps you strengthen many of your skills and abilities. If you don't know why you behave in certain ways, change is more difficult. For example, maybe you get in trouble for being loud in class. This might mean that you want attention from other people. Understanding this, you might be able to change and get attention in more positive ways.

Self-acceptance leads to honesty about your strengths and weaknesses. You know what these are because you are honestly looking at them. In this way, you build confidence in yourself. Self-acceptance means that you may not be perfect, but you can improve. Every teen with the courage to try can improve self-acceptance. Without self-acceptance, you'll be less effective and creative than you could be.

DID YOU KNOW?

Every year, alcohol or other drugs harm the health of thousands of teens. Many teens become pregnant, are killed in car crashes, or become infected with serious diseases including HIV/AIDS.

Seeking Acceptance From Outside

The pursuit of acceptance may drive teens to develop strong attitudes and behaviors. Many of these are normal, positive, and healthy. Sometimes, though, the lack of self-acceptance comes out in negative behaviors. Teens may seem irritable, sad, or confused. They may try to control their surroundings. Too often, teens are their own harshest critic. Self-criticisim can lead to self-rejection. Long-lasting feelings of self-rejection can trigger emotional depression and even thoughts of suicide.

Frequently, teens who can't accept themselves may desperately want friends to give them that acceptance. Teens may do just about anything to gain someone's approval.

Sometimes, the need for acceptance pushes teens to abuse tobacco, alcohol, or other drugs. The pressure to be accepted can be enormous. It can push teens to participate in sexual behaviors that can lead to unintended pregnancy or serious infections. It can push teens to make poor food choices, such as starving themselves to look thinner. They may go against their values. For example, take a look at Linda.

QUOTE

"No one can make you feel inferior without your consent."
—Eleanor Roosevelt

Linda, Age 16

Linda was at a party with some classmates. Her dad was an alcoholic, and Linda had no intention of ending up like him. But at the party, everyone else seemed to be drinking. She wanted to say no, but she wondered if people would laugh at her. She hated that. Against her better judgment, she took a bottle of beer that someone handed her.

When teens lack self-acceptance, they may expect their friends, family, or others to reject or hate them. This belief can prevent teens from allowing anyone to get close to them. They may abandon others before others have a chance to reject them. They might hope this will protect them.

In the search for self-acceptance, teens often compare themselves to others. There's always someone with more accomplishments. For example, people at school may seem more successful, talented, or beautiful.

However, what one person considers a wonderful accomplishment, another may not. For example, you may value and admire a talented athlete. Yet a friend may consider athletic talent totally unimportant.

Athletic ability is something about which people may disagree. One person may admire athletic ability. Another person may think it's not important.

Self-Assessments and Self-Acceptance

How well do you accept yourself? Try this self-assessment to find out. Self-assessments are tests that can help people know themselves better. There are many kinds of self-assessments. Some are based on years of medical research. Some may have items about knowledge, attitudes, or behavior. They might look at a person's risk for depression or alcoholism. They may include issues about body image.

Assessing yourself on occasion can help you see what you should change. The key is that only *you* interpret the information. Teens created the self-assessment on the next page. It will help you rate your self-acceptance.

What Is My Self-Acceptance?

Read items 1–12 below. On a separate piece of paper, write the number that describes you best for each item. Use this scale:

4 = Almost always   3 = Mostly   2 = Sometimes   1 = Hardly ever

1. I set realistic goals.	4	3	2	1
2. I develop my strengths.	4	3	2	1
3. I'm self-confident.	4	3	2	1
4. I'm proud of myself.	4	3	2	1
5. I can handle stress.	4	3	2	1
6. I can use positive self-talk.	4	3	2	1
7. I imagine being successful.	4	3	2	1
8. I develop supportive relationships.	4	3	2	1
9. I'm involved in school and community activities.	4	3	2	1
10. I know and express my feelings responsibly.	4	3	2	1
11. I'm responsible for my thoughts, feelings, and actions.	4	3	2	1
12. I find ways to grow.	4	3	2	1

Add up your points. The closer your total is to 48, the higher your self-acceptance probably is. For items on which you scored 2 or 1, think about ways to improve in those areas.

Points to Consider: AcceptanceMatters

How are self-acceptance and health related to each other?

How might high self-acceptance be positive?

How do you think low self-acceptance could be negative?

Do you think it's hardest for teens to achieve physical, social, or mental and emotional self-acceptance? Why?

Chapter Overview

Most people like some things about the way they look but not other things.

Nearly all health behaviors relate to self-acceptance.

Your relationship with yourself is the basis of self-esteem. Some teens may try to raise their self-esteem in appropriate or inappropriate ways.

CHAPTER 2

⚙

Physical Self-Acceptance

Look at yourself in the mirror. Do you like what you see? You probably like some things and not others. Maybe you believe you're a little too short or your smile needs improvement. You might call this physical side of you **BodyMatters**. You can develop the physical side of self-acceptance. Self-acceptance is being happy with who you are. One step to self-acceptance is to identify your feelings about your physical traits.

Bodily differences can account for as much as 1,000 resting calories every day. That means two people may eat the exact same amount of food and exercise the same amount. However, one person will use more calories than the other.

Health Behaviors

Nearly all health behaviors relate to self-acceptance. This doesn't mean that you have to have perfect physical, mental, emotional, or social health. However, taking care of your health becomes an important task for you.

The Centers for Disease Control and Prevention (CDC) is a U.S. government agency. The CDC names six areas as responsible for most deaths and injuries among U.S. teens. The desire to increase self-acceptance motivates many teens to use these behaviors.

1. Tobacco use, including cigarettes, cigars, pipes, and chewing tobacco

2. Alcohol and other drug use

3. Sexual behaviors resulting in HIV infection, other sexually transmitted diseases (STDs), or unintended pregnancy

4. Eating patterns that contribute to disease, such as choosing a high-fat diet or trying to control weight in unhealthy ways

5. Lack of physical activity

6. Behaviors that result in intentional or unintentional injury. Violence is an example of intentional injury. Many fires, drowning, and falls produce unintentional injuries.

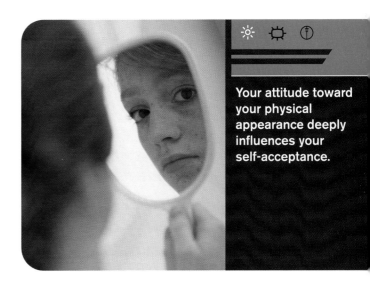

Your attitude toward your physical appearance deeply influences your self-acceptance.

Accepting Yourself

Often, teens don't accept their physical self. One major step in self-acceptance is the ability to take responsibility for yourself. Some teens want other people's opinion about their looks. In doing so, they may hope to feel better about themselves. Some teens want someone else to blame if they can't accomplish a goal.

You may see yourself accurately. However, your attitude is equally important. Look at Joseph. Is his view of himself accurate? Is it positive or negative? Should he change his self-acceptance?

Joseph, Age 15

Joseph had acne. During the year, it got so bad that his face hurt constantly. He let his hair grow long to help cover the pimples. He seldom looked up or smiled. Joseph told his friends that he looked so bad, no girl would want to date him.

As with Joseph and most teens, your physical appearance is probably important to you. Many people spend lots of money to change their physical appearance. They may hope to boost their self-acceptance by doing this. Try the self-assessment on the next page about accepting your physical appearance.

Physical Self-Acceptance

You'll be doing two things in this self-assessment. You'll rate how much you like your physical traits and how well you accept those same traits. Follow these steps.

Step 1 Read items 1–22 below, which show individual traits about you. On a separate piece of paper, write the number that shows how well you like each trait. Use this scale:

4 = It's great.   3 = It's fine.
2 = It could be better.   1 = It's terrible.

Step 2 Next to that first number on your paper, write the number that best shows how well you accept each trait. Use this scale:

4 = Very accepting   3 = Mostly accepting
2 = Somewhat accepting   1 = Not accepting

1. Hair color	4	3	2	1
2. Eye color	4	3	2	1
3. Skin color	4	3	2	1
4. Height	4	3	2	1
5. Weight	4	3	2	1
6. Face shape	4	3	2	1
7. Teeth	4	3	2	1
8. Smile	4	3	2	1
9. Nose	4	3	2	1

10. Hairstyle	4	3	2	1
11. Age	4	3	2	1
12. Feet	4	3	2	1
13. Hands	4	3	2	1
14. Chest or breast size	4	3	2	1
15. Neck size	4	3	2	1
16. Resistance to disease	4	3	2	1
17. Energy level	4	3	2	1
18. Physical stamina, or ability to do long-lasting exercise	4	3	2	1
19. Strength	4	3	2	1
20. Coordination	4	3	2	1
21. Musical ability	4	3	2	1
22. Voice	4	3	2	1

Add up your first set of numbers. Then add your second set of numbers. Subtract the lower total from the higher total. The closer you are to 0, the higher your physical self-acceptance probably is. Items with a 1 or 2 show traits you might need to work on accepting. Pay special attention to the traits that you can change. Some are more easily changed than others. Changing your hairstyle is probably easy. It's not so easy to change your height.

"My friend Jocie wanted a tattoo, but her parents wouldn't let her get one. So she took a needle and gave herself a tattoo on her ankle. It looked okay, but Jocie ended up getting a pretty bad infection and going to the hospital. Her doctor said he's heard of lots of kids trying that and ending up with all kinds of problems."—Haylee, age 14

Relate to Yourself

Your relationship to yourself is the most important of all. It's the basis of self-esteem. Teens may attempt to increase this respect for themselves appropriately. For example they may exercise or eat healthier snacks to shape their body. Sometimes they may try to raise their self-esteem inappropriately or illegally. They may take too many laxatives to lose weight, for instance. Or they may smoke to impress friends.

If teens fail to increase their self-esteem in appropriate ways, they may blame themselves for yet another failure. This latest failure is their inability to accept themselves. Some teens get into the habit of blaming others for their low self-esteem. This may begin a shift of blame from themselves to whoever is convenient. Take a look at Sondra, who hasn't been successful at losing weight.

Sondra, Age 17

Sondra took a bite of her candy bar and said, "My legs are so huge! I'll never get on the swim team looking like this! That dumb doctor! He told me to eat less, and it hasn't worked at all!"

Teens are under social and media pressure to have certain body shapes. This pressure often seems to apply only to females. But increasingly, today's males have similar pressure. For example, one brand of action figure first appeared in 1964. If the figure were 5 feet 10 inches tall (1.78 meters), his waist would have been 32 inches (80 centimeters). His biceps, the large muscle at the front of the upper arm, would have been 12 inches (30 centimeters). In 1991, the figure had changed. His waist shrank to 27 inches (68 centimeters). His biceps grew to 16 inches (40 centimeters). By 1998, the figure's waist would have been 36.5 inches (92.7 centimeters). His biceps grew to 27 inches (68 centimeters).

Sondra blamed her doctor when she thought she didn't lose enough weight. Yet she seems not to have followed his advice. Blaming others for your failures or weaknesses is unhealthy. So is blaming yourself for others' failures. When you blame yourself, you may give others permission to blame you, too.

We all can change how we view ourselves and others. Self-acceptance is powerful. Put it to work in positive ways.

Points to Consider: BodyMatters

Give an example of each of the three parts of self-acceptance.

What physical traits could you change? Rank the changes according to cost and how much they might risk your health.

How might accurate physical self-acceptance lead to positive health behavior?

Do you agree that self-acceptance is being happy with who you are? Why or why not?

Chapter Overview

The mental and emotional side of self-acceptance isn't always easy to see. It has to do with feelings, attitudes, and values.

Sharing negative feelings with people sometimes may be hard.

Perfectionists are less likely than other people to accept themselves.

Being happy isn't always easy. Some people believe they'll be happy only in the future. Self-accepting people try to live happily every day.

CHAPTER 3

Mental and Emotional Self-Acceptance

This chapter focuses on the relationship of self-acceptance to **MindMatters**, the mental and emotional part of health. The physical part of self-acceptance is clear. It has to do with your appearance and the health status of the body. But the mental and emotional part often is hidden. However, the feelings, attitudes, and values you have eventually will surface. They may show themselves in decisions, behaviors, and actions.

Clearly communicating feelings to other people is one characteristic of good mental and emotional self-acceptance.

What Is Mental and Emotional Self-Acceptance?

Mental and emotional self-acceptance means:

- Setting realistic short-term and long-term goals

- Having an optimistic and confident attitude toward challenges

- Recognizing reality

- Being curious about and interested in life

- Tolerating other people's differences

- Coping with change

- Taking positive risks

- Thinking clearly

- Communicating feelings

Someone with good mental and emotional self-acceptance usually can balance abilities and the demands on them. You can improve your mental and emotional self-acceptance by increasing your accomplishments and accepting reality. Increasing your accomplishments means trying and succeeding at something manageable and realistic. For example, imagine you've always wanted to learn sign language. How could you begin to be successful?

Accepting reality doesn't mean giving up your dreams. It might mean that you change them. Maybe you dream of wearing certain kinds of clothes. You may not be able to afford them if you're unwilling to take a part-time job. Be honest with yourself about who you are, what you want, and what you can do.

☀ ☼ ①

Trang, Age 13

"I don't speak Vietnamese, even though my grandfather is from Vietnam. I once told some friends I could speak it, and they thought that was cool. But I always worry that one of them will want me to say something or translate something. I know it's stupid to pretend like this, but it's too late to change now!"

Some people pretend they can do or become something when they really can't. This is not accepting reality. For example, perhaps you pretend you can become a professional athlete though you never practice. This may result in a dislike of yourself. You may blame yourself and others for your failure.

However, don't give up on your dreams too soon. Even if you can't do something now, it's often possible to gain the ability for the future. Did you know that baseball was Michael Jordan's best sport when he was young? Did you know that Walt Disney's first company went bankrupt before he sold his first animated cartoon?

A perfectionist teen may feel a powerful urge to continually rewrite assignments to meet unrealistic standards.

How Are You?

If you looked into a mirror and asked yourself how you are, what would you answer? When asked how they are, most people probably answer "Fine." This often isn't completely honest. Usually, people know when they're happy and why. There may be hundreds of reasons. Maybe things are going well at home or school. However, many people can't describe their feelings when they have problems.

How might your friends answer this question? Do you think some people don't want to hear the answer?

Sometimes, sharing negative thoughts or feelings is difficult because you don't wish to burden others. You may be afraid that others won't understand your feelings. Maybe others have put you down for expressing your thoughts or emotions. Some families, cultures, or genders may have more difficulty than others in communicating. It may take a long time and lots of courage to sort and share feelings.

Perfectionism and fear of failure are closely related. Sometimes a perfectionist won't try something if there's a chance that he or she won't do it perfectly. The perfectionist may believe it's better to do nothing at all than to try something and fail at it.

Who's Perfect?

An inability to share feelings may make people feel less than perfect. Not being perfect may cause problems for some people. Are you a perfectionist? This is someone who is unhappy about anything that doesn't meet extremely high standards or expectations. Look at these questions. If you answer yes to either one, you may be a perfectionist.

Do you redo your work so that everyone will think it's perfect?

Do you expect others to be perfect? Do you get angry if they aren't?

Do you have to be a perfectionist to achieve mental and emotional self-acceptance? No! Actually, the opposite may be true. Perfectionists sometimes worry too much about other people's opinion of them. People may value a perfectionist because they know the person will do a great job. People who accept themselves do care about their work, too. However, they also accept their mistakes.

What's Your Temperature?

A person's average temperature is 98.6 degrees Fahrenheit (37 degrees Celsius). Have you ever felt warm because you had a fever? If so, someone probably took your temperature. This information helped determine your treatment.

Some health professionals take your self-acceptance temperature. Instead of using a thermometer, the person may ask: "How are you?" or "Are you happy?" Your answer shows your mental and emotional temperature.

What's your mental and emotional self-acceptance temperature? Take this self-assessment to see if your temperature is normal, hot, or cold.

My Mental and Emotional Temperature

Read items 1–17 below. On a separate piece of paper, write the number that describes you best for each item. Use this scale:

3 = Almost always   2 = Sometimes   1 = Hardly ever

1. I pay attention to others and my surroundings.	3	2	1
2. I have self-respect and stand up for myself. I deserve to be happy.	3	2	1
3. I can deal with day-to-day challenges.	3	2	1
4. I seek knowledge and truth.	3	2	1
5. I seek to know myself better.	3	2	1
6. I accept that my attitudes, opinions, or feelings don't change facts.	3	2	1
7. I'm a good friend to myself.	3	2	1
8. I correct myself kindly and compassionately.	3	2	1

Self-Acceptance

"He who undervalues himself is justly
undervalued by others."
—William Hazlitt, English writer

9. I'm responsible for my actions.   **3**   **2**   **1**

10. I set short-term and long-term goals.   **3**   **2**   **1**

11. I use my intelligence and common sense
    productively.   **3**   **2**   **1**

12. I think for myself.   **3**   **2**   **1**

13. I'm assertive and express myself appropriately.   **3**   **2**   **1**

14. My behavior reflects my values and hopes.   **3**   **2**   **1**

15. I achieve my goals.   **3**   **2**   **1**

16. I delay immediate rewards and pleasures for the
    accomplishment of a long-range goal.   **3**   **2**   **1**

17. I'm trustworthy.   **3**   **2**   **1**

Add up your points. The closer your total is to 51, the more positive
your mental and emotional self-acceptance probably are. Items with a 1
may indicate some areas you can try to improve.

Happiness 101

You may think of mental and emotional self-acceptance as being happy with who you are. However, being happy with yourself is easy for some and difficult for others. Learning to be happy is a step in the direction of positive mental and emotional self-acceptance.

There's a common phrase: "Happiness isn't a destination. It's a way of travel." Most teens want to be happy. Many who search for happiness never find it. They see happiness as a place to end up someday in the years ahead. Have you heard anyone say, "I'd be happy if only I were older (or married, or had a job, or had more money)"?

Don't save all of your "happiness dollars" for the future. Accepting yourself mentally and emotionally means trying to live happily every day. Practice being happy and work hard to enjoy the journey you're on. It's mainly a matter of your attitude. Abraham Lincoln said, "Most folks are about as happy as they make up their minds to be."

Don't wait until some future date to be happy. Learn how to be happy every day.

Points to Consider: MindMatters

Have you ever felt afraid to share negative feelings with others? If so, were you ever able to share them? What happened?

Do you consider yourself a perfectionist? Why or why not?

Do you think it's true that you won't succeed if you pretend to be something you aren't? Explain.

Are you happy now, or do you hope to be happy later? How might your answer affect your choices now?

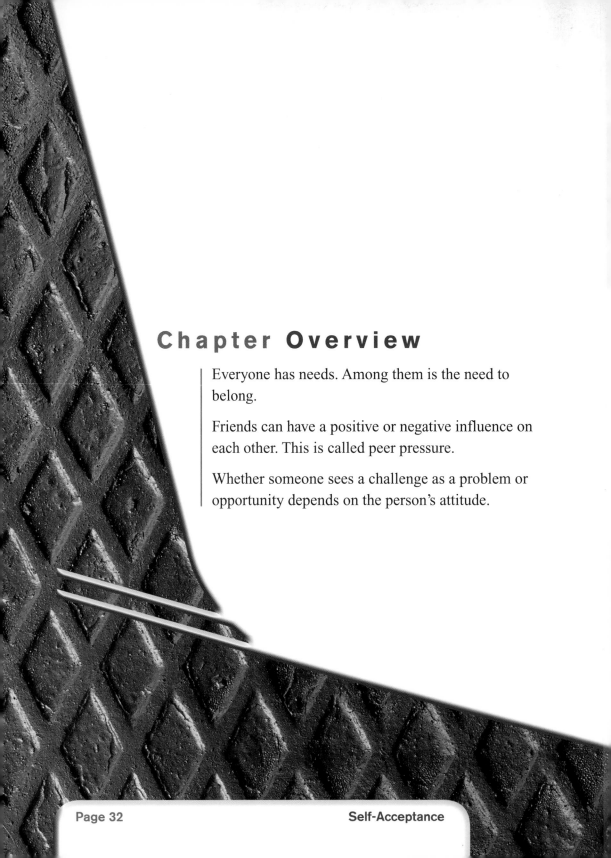

Chapter Overview

Everyone has needs. Among them is the need to belong.

Friends can have a positive or negative influence on each other. This is called peer pressure.

Whether someone sees a challenge as a problem or opportunity depends on the person's attitude.

CHAPTER 4

Social Self-Acceptance

How Well Do You Know You?

Most people want to be wise. An old saying sums up wisdom in two words, "Know thyself." You probably believe you know yourself. You know your likes and dislikes.

But have you looked deeper into your inner likes and dislikes? Knowing all sides of yourself, including your social side, will balance your self-acceptance. You can think of your relationships with others as **SocialMatters**. This chapter focuses on understanding and accepting the needs associated with our friends and relationships.

Your Needs

All humans, including you, have needs. Our needs motivate us to fulfill them. Some needs are more important than others. For example, basic physical needs such as food, water, and shelter are critical. Without these things, we might die.

People who won't act until they see what other people are doing may be struggling with low self-confidence.

Our needs are a little like steps. Once our basic physical needs are met, we can attempt to satisfy higher-level needs. Higher-level needs include belonging, relationships, achievement, confidence, recognition, and love.

What Do Your Friends See and Say?

One of the higher-level needs is belonging. One way to belong is to have friends. During the teen years, friendships can offer fun, companionship, comfort, and support. With friendships, you can learn things and develop good listening and other communication skills. Self-acceptance can help you gain and maintain friendships. However, to have good friends, you must be a good friend. Accepting yourself is an important first step in developing friendships.

Have you ever seen a classmate make a decision by looking around to see what others are doing? That person may be struggling with low self-esteem or lack of confidence. However, over time, this behavior can become a habit, and the struggles with self-acceptance can grow. This can result in the inability to stand up for one's own values and convictions.

Self-Acceptance

DID YOU KNOW?

You can improve your social life by being alone. Before you can accept yourself, you must know yourself. One way to know yourself is through time alone. It gives you the opportunity to think about yourself and others. Within even a short time, some people can solve problems that have bothered them for a long time.

If you want others to admire and respect you, you must behave admirably and respectably. However, what your friends think of you and how they accept you may affect your thoughts, feelings, and behaviors. This peer pressure can be positive or negative. Being part of a group that exerts positive peer pressure can improve your self-esteem. Peer pressure can encourage you not to give up on your dreams. It can improve your health, grades, or team.

Jimmie, Age 16

The basketball team had a meeting at school. Afterward, the players went out for pizza. As they walked, Jimmie pulled out some cigarettes. He started to light one, but several of the other players protested. "Oh man, don't put that dumb-looking thing in your mouth!" "Yeah, you want to get kicked off the team?" "Jimmie, you're crazy. Are you trying to die of cancer like my uncle did?"

Jimmie hesitated, then he said, "I guess you're right." He decided to throw away the pack.

Negative peer pressure can involve you in dangerous or illegal behavior. You may feel pressure to go against your values. You may jeopardize your future goals and plans. For instance, some teens choose to use alcohol because they're afraid of what their friends might say. They might achieve their goals better by setting their own values and standards of behavior.

Are you a good friend? Use this self-assessment to test whether you have what it takes to be a good friend.

Your Friendship Scale

Read items 1–12 below. On a separate piece of paper, write the number that describes you best for each item. Use this scale:

3 = Most of the time   2 = Sometimes   1 = Rarely

1. I encourage my friends to be their best.	3	2	1
2. My friends can count on me.	3	2	1
3. I avoid asking my friends to do dangerous or illegal things.	3	2	1
4. I avoid putting my friends down.	3	2	1
5. I understand my friends' feelings and emotions.	3	2	1
6. I'm attentive and considerate of my friends' feelings and emotions.	3	2	1
7. I care about my friends.	3	2	1
8. My friends and I have common values and ethics.	3	2	1
9. I'm honest with my friends.	3	2	1
10. I'm a good listener with my friends.	3	2	1
11. I can compromise with my friends.	3	2	1
12. I understand and support my friends' talents.	3	2	1

Add up your points. The closer your total is to 36, the more qualities of a good friend you have. Consider working on and improving the areas in which you scored 1 or 2 points.

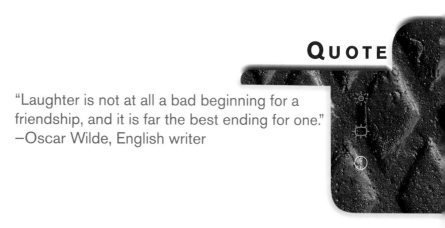

Opportunity or Problem?

Self-accepting people often see problems as opportunities. People who are less self-confident may see those same opportunities as problems. For example, they may dwell on their mistakes or those of others. They may feel they have no control, or they may see themselves as victims. Perhaps they have a history of being put down. It may take a lot of encouragement from others to move in a positive, healthy direction.

Do you see problems or opportunities? It's all in your attitude. Negative experiences don't have to ruin your dreams, goals, or plans for success. The key is to focus on how you react. If the situation has bad results, learn from it but don't dwell on it. You may experience temporary setbacks. That doesn't mean that you can't succeed.

There's a saying: "When life deals you lemons, make lemonade." Now may be the time to focus on your stengths and on the positive aspects in your life.

You might be better able to accept certain difficult situations. Maybe you need a way to look at them from a new or different perspective. Do you ask others what they think? Your social self-acceptance and self-esteem are closely related. Here are 10 yes-or-no questions to help you determine your social self-acceptance.

Social Self-Acceptance

On a separate sheet of paper, write your answers to items 1–10.

Do you believe your parents:

1. Think well of you?	**Yes**	**No**
2. Are proud of you?	**Yes**	**No**
3. Love you?	**Yes**	**No**

Do you believe your friends:

4. Accept you?	**Yes**	**No**
5. Respect you?	**Yes**	**No**
6. Enjoy you?	**Yes**	**No**
7. Encourage you?	**Yes**	**No**

Do you:

8. Make negative statements about yourself?	**Yes**	**No**
9. Wish you were different?	**Yes**	**No**
10. Let others push you into doing things that you don't want to do?	**Yes**	**No**

If you answer no to questions 1–7, your beliefs about how others see you may lower your self-acceptance. If you answer yes to questions 8–10, you might need to raise your self-acceptance and self-esteem. You could do this by saying positive instead of negative things about yourself. You could show others that you value your own opinions of yourself.

Having supportive friends can help raise your social self-acceptance.

Points to Consider: SocialMatters

Is it important to know yourself? Why or why not?

What do you believe are the three most important characteristics of a good friend? Why?

Give an example of positive peer pressure. Give an example of negative peer pressure.

When you face a challenge, do you usually think of it as a problem or an opportunity? How does this attitude affect your behavior?

Chapter Overview

Everyone has both gifts and disabilities. Disabilities may have serious consequences.

Sometimes people feel angry about, disbelieving about, or afraid of disabilities.

The way people label themselves and others can affect their self-acceptance.

Some people see their talents as disabilities because they are embarrassed or afraid they won't be accepted.

Several examples of real people show that disabilities can be overcome.

CHAPTER 5

The Exceptional Side of Self-Acceptance

Gifted or Disabled?

We all possess exceptional gifts and traits. Perhaps we have the gift of being caring, kind, and giving. Perhaps we have physical gifts such as being good at music, art, or athletics. Maybe we have superior math, science, or other learning traits.

On the other hand, we're all disabled to some degree. We may be disabled physically, mentally, emotionally, or socially. Our disability may come from physical or environmental factors. It may result from our own actions or those of others. As with gifts, disabilities may be associated with music, art, learning, athletics, relationships, or emotions. This can be called **ExceptionalMatters**.

Sam and Tisha, Age 15

Sam is good looking, popular, and athletic. However, he had an accident that put him in a wheelchair. Since then, he hasn't been able to get a date. Tisha is also good looking, but she has few friends. She spends much of her time studying and doing school projects. That hard work shows in her excellent grades. Most of the people who talk with her are only interested in getting answers to homework assignments. Tisha wonders if guys think she's too smart.

Having a disability doesn't mean you're inferior or incapable or should give up. It also doesn't mean you should receive special favors. How you support or recognize the abilities of others or yourself creates greater understanding and self-acceptance. You can, however, learn about symptoms, characteristics, and treatments for disabilities. That knowledge may help you become more informed, skilled, understanding, and comfortable about them. Differences in appearance, emotions, or intellect may offer opportunities to appreciate the many sides of people.

Self-Acceptance

Many children from stress-filled families experience failure from the earliest stages of life. They come to believe that they are meant to fail and that the future holds little for them. They may believe they have little to lose by using negative behavior. They may drop out of school, use drugs, commit violent crimes, or have babies at a young age.

Consequences of Disabilities

Some teens experience serious physical, emotional, or sexual abuse or neglect. These experiences can slow appropriate development. Sometimes these factors contribute to high-risk behaviors. About a million U.S. teens become pregnant each year. About half of these girls give birth. In 1997, around 79 percent of U.S. students drank alcohol. About 31 percent of those students drank before age 13. The number of teens with mental and emotional disorders is on the rise.

Unfortunately, many of these difficulties lead to serious, disabling consequences. Teens in these situations come from all communities, families, and ethnic and racial groups. Teens from well-meaning families also can be in stressful situations. In some homes, the pressure to perform academically or athletically results in unhealthy responses. These might include extreme weight loss, depression, or lack of sleep.

Alisha, Age 14

Alisha had been having trouble in math and science. Her parents told her she better straighten up. But it seemed like the harder she tried, the worse her grades became. The only person who seemed to care about how she felt was her boyfriend. He had been pushing for sex lately. Alisha didn't want to have sex, but she was worried that he would dump her if she kept refusing. If she lost him, she'd be all alone with her troubles.

Sorting Out Emotions

Disabilities often bring many feelings with them. You may be angry about a disability. Maybe you or a friend has been in a serious accident. Perhaps it changes the way you're involved in an activity that you used to do well.

You may be disbelieving about a disability, especially if it's not obvious. Accepting a disability might be easier if a person is in a wheelchair or uses sign language. Many people with disabilities, however, look like most people. For example, what does a learning disability look like? Sometimes, a disability may seem like an excuse for being lazy, acting out in class, or not doing homework.

You may be afraid of a disability. You may fear not knowing what to say or how to act with someone who has a disability. You may fear somehow "catching" the disability. You may fear being put down because you're associating with someone outside your usual circle of friends. Fear often results from lack of knowledge.

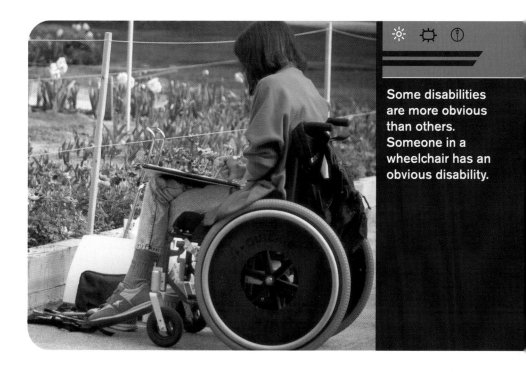

Some disabilities are more obvious than others. Someone in a wheelchair has an obvious disability.

Some teens with disabilities may not look like others. Physically, they may rely on technology to accomplish tasks that others take for granted. Issues related to health and disability can be complicated.

The labels you hear about yourself can stir up both positive and negative emotions. For example, how do these labels make you feel?

Bad	Hostile	Stupid
Bold	Imaginative	Tender
Boring	Logical	Ugly
Brave	Repulsive	Useless
Confident	Responsible	Weak
Courteous	Sexy	Wonderful
Enthusiastic	Silly	Worthy
Helpful	Skilled	Youthful

"Your life is like a piece of paper on which every passerby leaves a mark."—Chinese proverb

Self-acceptance isn't only about how others label us. It's also about how we label ourselves. Some of the terms on the previous page probably give you negative feelings, some positive feelings. Which ones describe you? This will give you another glimpse of your self-acceptance.

Other people can greatly influence a person's self-acceptance. One way is by labeling each other. Do we use embarrassing terms? Do we use respectful, confidence-building terms? Using positive terms about others has a double benefit. It can help increase others' self-esteem and can help develop and maintain friendships.

Barriers to Understanding

Sometimes, how we treat others creates a barrier to their being fully understood or accepted. Maybe we tease them beyond their ability to understand we're joking. Maybe they're afraid to tell you they are in an abusive relationship. Maybe they don't recognize the danger from alcohol or other drugs. Rather than encouraging a classmate to develop musical, athletic, or academic talents, maybe we're a bit jealous.

Some people view their talents or abilities as disabilities. Because they want to fit in with their peers, they may minimize their gifts or hide them completely.

Mychal was an excellent student. His teacher wanted Mychal to take some advanced classes at a nearby college. Mychal's friends already teased him for being "too smart." He told his teacher he didn't want to take the classes.

Later, and with lots of support, Mychal may recognize his friends' label as a barrier to self-acceptance. For now, he chooses to remain silent and hope no one will notice his gifts.

Overcoming Disabilities

A disability may be called a deviance, abnormality, or disease. Most of these terms mean "unacceptable" or "unequal." Some people have difficulty seeing past others' disabilities. Many people have overcome the limitations that society has traditionally seen as a disability. Look at these examples.

James Earl Jones had a stuttering problem as a young man. He went on to become the imposing voice of Darth Vader in several *Star Wars* movies.

Ludwig van Beethoven was a great musician. His poor reading skills might be a reading disability called dyslexia today. An inability to focus might be called attention deficit disorder (ADD). Later in life, he also became deaf, but still he wrote some of his best-known works.

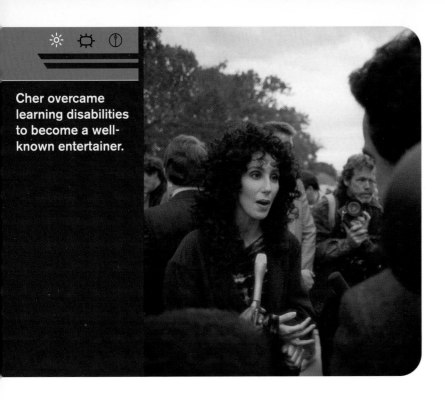

Cher overcame learning disabilities to become a well-known entertainer.

Thomas Edison was taken out of school because he was such a poor student. His mother taught him at home. As an adult, he created thousands of inventions.

George Washington couldn't spell well when he was young, and his grammar was poor.

Tom Cruise had severe reading problems throughout his school years. Yet, he was able to memorize lines and has successfully performed on the stage and in many movies.

Albert Einstein was a slow talker. Even as an adult, Einstein found searching for words to be a problem. He found schoolwork difficult and failed an exam in electrical engineering in high school. His work on relativity revolutionized modern physics.

Cher has become a musical and screen star despite learning disabilities.

Henry Winkler is famous for his role as Fonzie in the TV show *Happy Days*. He has directed many movies despite learning disabilities.

Self-Acceptance

Albert Einstein had problems in school when he was a young man.

Points to Consider: ExeceptionalMatters

How do you feel when you meet someone with a disability? Explain.

Have you ever pretended you couldn't do something? Why or why not?

This chapter mentions several famous people who have disabilities. Choose one you admire and explain why.

Chapter Overview

We can think about making changes in our life. But until we actually act, nothing will change.

To handle challenges in life, you can follow some tips to build your self-acceptance.

You're an important influence on the children in your life. You can work to be a good example.

It's hard to get anywhere if you don't have goals in life.

CHAPTER 6

Self-Acceptance in Action

The Latin term *carpe diem* means "Seize the day." Make the most of each moment. Life is a journey with ups and downs. You succeed, fail, act, react, laugh, cry, learn, and grow. But rarely do you stay the same. Now it's time to put what you have learned about self-acceptance into action. Your decisions and behaviors can enhance your life and possibly the life of others. Self-acceptance means that you can recognize and take healthy, positive actions for you. This recognition might be called **WisdomMatters**.

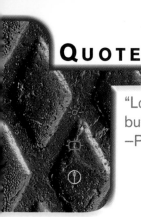

QUOTE

"Long-range planning does not deal with future decisions but with the future of present decisions."
–Peter F. Drucker, American writer

Ernesto, Age 14

Ernesto sat on the couch, staring at the TV screen. He looked at the soda in one hand and the chips in the other. He thought, "Being a couch potato isn't healthy. I suppose I ought to get up, cross the room, and turn off the TV. Then I should put this junk food away and get some exercise." He was about to stand up. But just then, the theme music for the cartoon "CatVentures" came on. Ernesto relaxed again and said to himself, "I can always start exercising tomorrow."

Change Today

You can change a room by painting walls or hanging posters. You can change your life the same way. With a room, you can read and get advice about how to change it. However, nothing will change until you put something on the wall. Likewise, you can read and get advice about how to change your life. But until you put your desires into action, nothing will change. Decide what you want to change today so tomorrow is better!

Building Self-Acceptance Skills

Each day brings new adventures and challenges. The higher your self-acceptance, the easier the journey, even with scary or difficult events. Here are some tips for building your self-acceptance.

No one is perfect. Beginning musicians must practice to become better.

1. Know yourself and your beliefs. Most people focus on the things they dislike about themselves. Begin to focus on the things you like about yourself. Focusing on the positive can help raise your self-esteem and self-acceptance.

2. Begin self-honesty. One of the first rules to building self-acceptance is to be honest with yourself. Some teens cover up what they know and believe about themselves until they no longer know the truth.

3. Do the best you can. Remember, no one is perfect. Aim to learn from mistakes, but don't dwell on them. The best people in any field begin with basics. New basketball players can't always get the ball in the basket. Musicians struggle to find the notes. But they practice and slowly improve. Having abilities is largely combining the goal with practice.

4. Be a good listener. Communication with self and others is important in building self-acceptance. A good listener encourages the other speaker and doesn't interrupt. As a listener, always focus on what the other person is saying. Don't think about what you are going to be saying next.

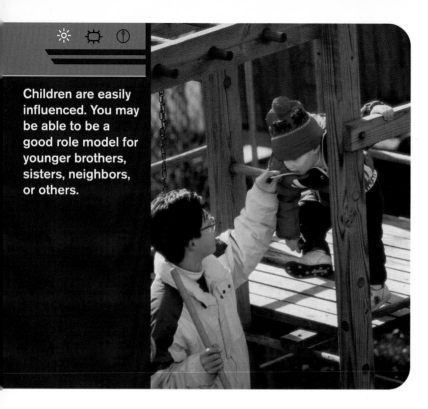

Children are easily influenced. You may be able to be a good role model for younger brothers, sisters, neighbors, or others.

5. Don't give up on yourself. Be willing to try new things. Be willing to risk not succeeding. Stretch your skills. Perhaps you try five new things. Three don't go so well, two go terrific. You now have two more abilities. As you add abilities, you can become more confident. Your confidence allows you to continue to try new things and accept a failed attempt occasionally.

6. Define yourself. Don't try to be someone you're not. Most teens are trying to improve themselves and be a better person. Perhaps you want to be more honest or less jealous. You may need help from others to recognize your talents and faults. Getting rid of faults is difficult and takes hard work. It even can be painful. By defining yourself, you can better fit your actions to your beliefs.

7. Be a good self-acceptance role model. Self-acceptance is contagious! You may have younger brothers, sisters, cousins, other relatives, or neighbors whom you care about. You're an important influence in helping the development of their self-acceptance.

Think of times when you are involved with children. Are you a positive or negative influence on their self-acceptance? Here's a quick way to check.

Children Need a Role Model

On a separate sheet of paper, write your answers to items 1–10.

1. Do you help children find their abilities?	Yes	No
2. Do you help them develop these abilities?	Yes	No
3. Do you provide as many normal and successful experiences as possible?	Yes	No
4. Do you provide emotional support?	Yes	No
5. Are you patient?	Yes	No
6. Do you respect their right to have their own ideas and opinions?	Yes	No
7. Do you help them understand that being different is okay?	Yes	No
8. Do you help them learn to deal with their feelings?	Yes	No
9. Do you help them learn how to treat other people?	Yes	No
10. Do you help them learn to be forgiving?	Yes	No

The more times you answer yes, the more you're contributing to children's positive self-acceptance.

Did You Know?

Don't give up. Look at events from the life of <u>Abraham Lincoln.</u>

1832 Ran for Illinois state legislature and lost.

1834 Ran for state legislature and won.

1838 Ran for speaker of the state legislature and lost.

1840 Reelected to Illinois legislature.

1846 Ran for U.S. Congress and won.

1849 Denied appointment as land officer.

1854 Ran for U.S. Senate and lost.

1858 Ran for U.S. Senate and lost again.

1860 Elected president of the United States.

What's Your Destination?

Each day brings decisions that can take you far from where you want to be. To reach your goals, you need to know what they are. Do you believe that where you end up depends on others or maybe just luck? Do you feel that you have no control over where you end up? If you feel you have no destination, now is the time to change!

Here is a list of possible life goals, or destinations. Rank them in order of importance to you. Feel free to change your mind as you go along. The end result should indicate your life's goals.

Comfort

Excitement

Financial security

Freedom and free choice

Happiness

Pleasure

Self-respect

Sense of accomplishment

True friendships

Wisdom

Understanding yourself is the basis for self-acceptance. Goals give you a direction and focus. Do your decisions and behaviors contribute to your life's priorities? The greater your understanding, the higher likelihood for a healthy self-acceptance. Completing these statements can help you understand yourself better.

1. I'm proud that I:

2. Something I'm getting better at is:

3. My greatest strength is:

4. I have the power to:

5. I get in trouble when I:

6. I get praised when I:

7. I want to be able to:

8. I have difficulty dealing with:

9. If I want to, I can:

10. I can help other people to:

Work on accepting yourself. Then put your self-acceptance into action.

Self-Acceptance

When you understand yourself, you'll have better self-acceptance. Put that knowledge to work.

Points to Consider: WisdomMatters

What does "seize the day" mean to you? How could you practice this in your life?

How is knowing how to change your life different from actually doing something to change it?

Do you think it's true that people can learn only by making mistakes? Why or why not?

Choose your most important life goal from the list on page 57. Why do you think it's the most important one?

NOTE

At publication, all resources listed here were accurate and appropriate to the topics covered in this book. Addresses and phone numbers may change. When visiting Internet sites and links, use good judgment. Remember, never give personal information over the Internet.

Internet Sites

Canadian Health Network
www.canadian-health-network.ca/customtools/homee.html
Links to health topics in Canada

Do Something
www.dosomething.org
Ideas for teens on setting goals and getting grants to help start volunteer projects

Go Ask Alice!
www.goaskalice.columbia.edu
Factual answers to questions about physical, emotional, spiritual, and sexual health

Kids Health for Teens
www.kidshealth.org/teen/index.html
Helpful information on mind and body matters for teens

Hot Line

National Domestic Violence Hot Line
1-800-799-7233
(24 hours a day, in English and Spanish)

Useful Addresses

Search Institute
700 South Third Street, Suite 210
Minneapolis, MN 55125-1138
1-800-888-7828
www.search-institute.org
Nonprofit organization that explores young
people's needs

Students Against Destructive Decisions
(SADD)
PO Box 800
Marlborough, MA 01752
www.saddonline.com
Provides surveys and information to help teens
lead a safe and happy life

For Further Reading

Covey, Sean. *The Seven Habits of Highly Effective Teens: The Ultimate Teenage Success Guide.*
New York: Fireside, 1998.

McCoy, Kathy, and Charles Wibbelsman. *Life Happens: A Teenager's Guide to Friends, Failure,
Sexuality, Love, Rejection, Addiction, Peer Pressure, Families, Loss, Depression, Change,
and Other Challenges of Living.* New York: Perigee, 1996.

Wandberg, Robert. *Creative Problem Solving: What's a Better Way?* Mankato, MN: Capstone, 2001.

Wandberg, Robert. *Self-Direction: Taking Positive Risks, Following Your Dreams.* Mankato, MN:
Capstone, 2001.

Glossary

arrogant (AR-uh-guhnt)—thinking oneself to be better than others

calorie (KAL-uh-ree)—a measurement of the amount of energy that certain activities use

competence (KAHM-puh-tuhnss)—the ability to handle life's routine and occasional challenges

confidence (KAHN-fuh-duhnss)—faith in yourself and your competence

disability (diss-uh-BIL-uh-tee)—a physical, mental, emotional, or social characteristic that may be seen as a challenge or a barrier

exceptional (ek-SEP-shuhn-uhl)—out of the ordinary

peer pressure (PEER PRESH-uhr)—the influence that people have on their friends; peer pressure can be positive or negative.

perfectionist (pur-FEK-shuhn-ist)—someone who is or becomes displeased with anything that isn't perfect or doesn't meet extremely high standards or expectations

priority (prye-OR-uh-tee)—a goal

self-acceptance (SELF-ak-SEP-tuhnss)—the ability to like and value yourself

self-esteem (SELF-ess-TEEM)—the respect people have for themselves

suicide (SOO-uh-side)—intentionally killing oneself

value (VAL-yoo)—standard, idea, or quality that a person considers to be important

visualize (VIZH-oo-uh-lize)—to imagine or think about something

Index

Index Continued

"Soaring to New Heights"